IMAGES
*of America*

# STUTTGART

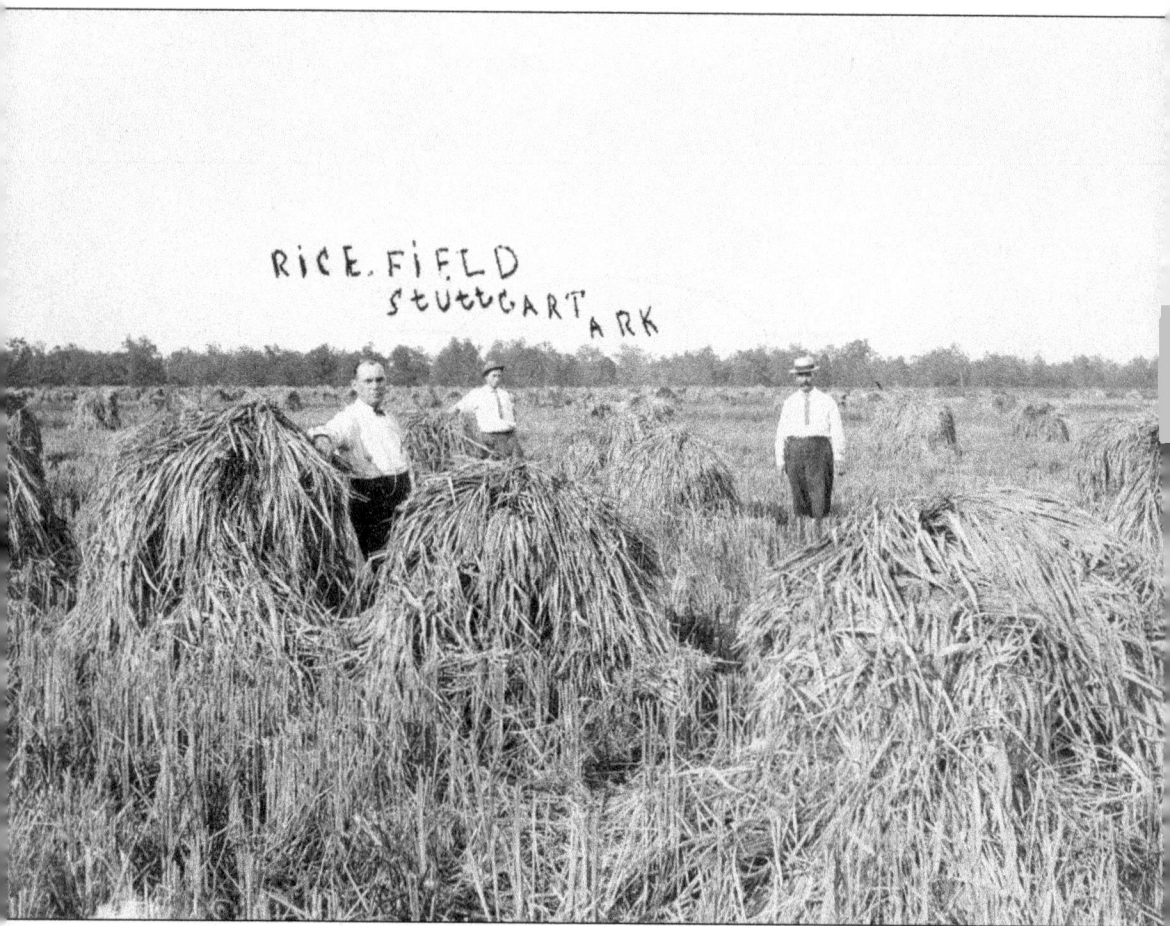

In the first years of rice production on the Grand Prairie, the crop was harvested using binders, which cut the rice plants and left them on the ground in bundles. Farmers then stacked the bundles into shocks and spread one bundle around the top, to shield the remainder from rain. The rice was left to dry before being threshed. (Courtesy of the Museum of the Arkansas Grand Prairie.)

ON THE COVER: Stuttgart sportsmen Kenneth "Slick" McCollum (left) and Louis "Red" Wilhelm pose for this quintessential duck hunting publicity photograph in flooded hardwoods typical of the region. McCollum, the 1939 duck calling contest winner, owned the highly successful Stuttgart Hunting Club along Bayou Meto. Wilhelm was the 1946 world champion duck caller. (Courtesy of the Museum of the Arkansas Grand Prairie.)

IMAGES
of America

# STUTTGART

Glenn Mosenthin

ARCADIA
PUBLISHING

Published by Arcadia Publishing
Charleston, South Carolina


Library of Congress Control Number: 2015931479

For all general information, please contact Arcadia Publishing:
Telephone 843-853-2070
Fax 843-853-0044
E-mail sales@arcadiapublishing.com
For customer service and orders:
Toll-Free 1-888-313-2665

Visit us on the Internet at www.arcadiapublishing.com

*To all the history-minded citizens who have given their time and efforts to preserve the unique heritage of the Stuttgart area*

# CONTENTS

# ACKNOWLEDGMENTS

This book is the result of a community effort. The author would like to thank everyone who assisted along the way with the project of accumulating images. The Museum of the Arkansas Grand Prairie in Stuttgart provided unlimited access to its photograph collection. Founded in 1974, the museum and its volunteers have contributed countless hours to preserve the area's history. Museum director Melanie Baden and archivist Gena Seidenschwarz were most hospitable in sharing knowledge and providing a "base of operations" for the author.

Another large image source was the Amici Club Collection at Stuttgart Public Library. Access to this treasure trove was graciously provided by the club's historians and Clara Jane Ahrens of the library. Specific thanks also go to senior archivist Brian Robertson of the Butler Center for Arkansas Studies; archivists Elizabeth Freeman and Mary Dunn of the Arkansas History Commission; Lynn Gamma and Samuel Shearin of the Air Force Heritage Research Agency; Stephanie Fischer of the *Stuttgart Daily Leader*; Terri Synco Maier of Emanuel Lutheran Church; Calvin and Bronwyn Criner of the Holman Heritage Community Center; Carl Humphrey of Stuttgart Municipal Airport; Andy Holbert of Little Rock; and Stuttgart residents Myrtle Sampson Welch, Mrs. B.T. Releford, Kay and Travis Trice, Lynn Keller, and Bill Bracewell.

The author would also like to thank his title manager at Arcadia Publishing, Jesse Darland, for support and guidance throughout the process. Finally, to all the historians in the various heritage groups around Stuttgart and the Arkansas Grand Prairie—thanks for all your contributions toward preserving our community's history. Many of the images in this volume appear courtesy of the Museum of the Arkansas Grand Prairie (MAGP) and the Amici Club, whose collection is maintained at the Stuttgart Public Library (AC/SPL).

# INTRODUCTION

The history of Stuttgart, Arkansas, began when a colony of German Lutherans arrived in 1878, led by a minister with visions of establishing a new church synod. Rev. Adam Buerkle, a native of Plattenhardt, Germany, settled near Woodville, Ohio, around 1867. He journeyed to the Arkansas Grand Prairie in 1878 to look for the right place to start a colony and found the prairie much to his liking. He purchased the antebellum Gum Pond Plantation, over 7,700 acres in size, for around $3 per acre. Reverend Buerkle brought two colonies to Gum Pond, one in 1878 and the other the following year, totaling around 28 families in all, including 17 Lutheran ministers. Buerkle sold half the plantation to his colonists for the same money he had paid and kept the other half for his family. It is unclear whether he occupied the original plantation house or built a new one on the site. His home also served as the church until 1896, when a permanent one was built.

Reverend Buerkle established a post office in his home in 1880, naming it Stuttgart after the city near his birthplace. School was held in the Buerkle home until a one-room schoolhouse was built around 1882 in what is today's business district. In 1883, the Texas & St. Louis (Cotton Belt) Railroad was completed through the Grand Prairie but ran some distance south of the Buerkle home. The railroad would not recognize Stuttgart as a stop since there was no post office present. Besides, the Cotton Belt was promoting Goldman as the new town at the time. Reverend Buerkle solved that problem by building a post office next to the tracks, and thus began Stuttgart on the present site. The new town was platted in 1884, but some years would pass before any real growth occurred.

The 1887 arrival of developer Thomas H. Leslie began the first era of expansion. Leslie had the business sense and ability to raise money necessary for the town's industrial growth. He founded a bank and built a railroad to Gillett to tap the region's resources. Leslie organized a real estate exchange that spurred trade in the business district. Stuttgart was incorporated in 1889, with Col. Robert Crockett, grandson of the famous Davy Crockett, elected as its first mayor. In the same year, both a preparatory college and new public school were built. Hay and cattle were the area's main income sources at the time. To encourage an industrial base for Stuttgart, promoters attracted businesses such as furniture makers, livery stables, flour and feed mills, gristmills, wagonmakers, farm implement factories, well drillers, dairies, blacksmith shops, and a concrete plant.

A dramatic chapter in Stuttgart's history began in 1902, when a successful rice crop was grown in the vicinity. By 1907, Arkansas's first rice mill was built, and in a mere two years, it needed to be expanded. Rice production took off in a big way, made viable by the prairie's clay soil layer, which supported irrigation. This attracted hundreds of settlers from the Midwest, who responded to advertising by promoters including J.E. Balle, W.M. Price, D.C. Adams, Philip Reinsch, Ray O. Burks, and Elliott Tallman, who organized twice-monthly railroad excursions to Stuttgart. The town experienced a boom, resulting in a new brick public school and railroad depot, sidewalks, sewers, a paved Main Street with many new brick buildings, and electricity to all homes.

After World War I, the price of rice dropped, causing growers to form a cooperative to gain greater dominance in the marketplace. They received cash advances on delivery of rice at harvesttime, instead of settling for low prices. Formed in 1921, the Arkansas Rice Growers Cooperative Association developed into today's Riceland Foods, the world's largest rice miller and marketer. The Rice Carnival was held in Stuttgart most years from 1909 to 1928. By the 1920s, area farms cultivated hundreds of thousands of acres of rice, which were flooded after the autumn harvest. With an abundance of surface water, nutritious flooded rice fields, and a convenient Mississippi Flyway location, millions of migratory waterfowl began wintering in the region. Grand Prairie residents quickly realized the opportunities commercial duck hunting would provide for their area. Lodges, guiding services, and suppliers were established, aiding the area's economy then just as today. The Depression years proved difficult for Stuttgart, but the founding of a new sporting competition would soon begin to transition the town to better times.

The first National Duck Calling Contest, sponsored by the local American Legion post, was held in November 1936. The event was inspired by a dispute that broke out among local duck hunters as to which one was the best caller. A committee of three Stuttgart Legionnaires—Thad McCollum, Dr. H.V. Glenn, and Verne Tindall—originated the contest. A carnival was set up on Main Street to accompany the annual contests, reviving the rice carnivals of previous years. The event, now known as the World Championship Duck Calling Contest, has grown to become a truly national and international competition. It is now part of the Wings Over the Prairie Festival, a huge source of revenue for the Stuttgart area and one of the largest such events in Arkansas.

In 1943, Producers Rice Mill was founded, and later expanded into cooperative rice drying. It is now one of the largest private-label packers of rice in the country. The World War II years brought another economic boost in the form of a military base. The Stuttgart Army Airfield operated from 1942 to 1945, performing flight training initially in the Waco Hadrian glider and then in twin-engine aircraft. The air base consisted of four 5,000-foot runways and facilities for 6,000 personnel. New houses were built to accommodate the influx of service personnel, while many residents rented out rooms. German and Italian prisoners of war housed at the airfield assisted area farmers with planting and harvest. After closure, the facility was deeded to Stuttgart and has since been operated as a municipal airport. In 1959, a three-mile Sports Car Club of America road course was laid out on the site, using the airport's runways and aprons. The Grand Prairie Grand Prix was held annually until 1978.

A.R. Thorell and Jacob Hartz Sr. introduced soybeans to area farmers in 1925 as a source of income and soil replenishment. However, it was not until after World War II, when combines and dryers became available, that the crop was successful on a large scale. In 1958, Arkansas Grain Corporation was formed to process, store, and market soybeans. The organization was merged in 1970 with Arkansas Rice Growers Cooperative, and the name Riceland Foods was adopted. The Stuttgart Industrial Development Corporation was formed in 1956 to draw new business ventures to the city, which then had 9,000 residents. By the 1960s, the city boasted a new shoe factory, hospital, waterworks, armory-auditorium building, city hall, library, and soybean oil plant, among many other improvements. Lennox Industries built a manufacturing plant in 1974, which remains a major local employer. Stuttgart today maintains its reputation as a progressive city and the "Rice and Duck Capital of the World."

# One

# FROM LUTHERAN COLONY TO PRAIRIE TOWN

In 1881, Berthold Reinsch opened the first general store in the vicinity of what became Stuttgart. This early photograph shows the B. Reinsch and Company Mercantile Store near present-day Buerkle and Washington Streets. The enterprise was later moved into Stuttgart and located at 208–210 South Main Street. Instead of money, the Reinsch Store issued chips, which were accepted all over the area. (MAGP.)

Rev. George Adam Buerkle is considered the founder of Stuttgart. He was born 1825 in Plattenhardt, Germany, and married Barbara Roth there. In 1852, they emigrated to America. After residing 26 years in Pennsylvania, Michigan, and Ohio, Reverend Buerkle traveled to Arkansas in 1878 to find a suitable location for a colony of Lutheran parishioners. The city of Stuttgart grew from this humble beginning. (Courtesy of Emanuel Lutheran Church.)

This view of Stuttgart from the northwest was apparently photographed from the Buerkle homestead near Gum Pond, west of the present-day hospital. Emanuel Lutheran Church is visible in the foreground, dating this image to between 1896 and 1902, when it was located on North Buerkle Road. The large building behind and to the left of the church is one of Stuttgart's early sawmills. (AC/SPL.)

This very early photograph depicts the west side of Main Street, between Third and Fourth Streets, in 1889. The buildings are, from right to left, Col. Robert Crockett's home, Simmons Land Office, T.V. Nicholson Paint Store, J.W. Searan Grocery, and J.T. White Grocery. (Courtesy of the Arkansas History Commission.)

Col. Robert Hamilton Crockett was a grandson of Davy Crockett. Born at Paris, Tennessee, in 1832, he became a successful lawyer in New Orleans and Memphis. He moved to Arkansas County in 1856, first settling at Crocketts Bluff, where he continued as an attorney and raised a company of Confederate troops during the Civil War. Later, he served as a legislator and was the first mayor of Stuttgart. (AC/SPL.)

Rural Scene on Grand Prairie.    Stuttgart, Ark.

This early postcard view depicts the area around Stuttgart, as it appeared when settlers from the Midwest began arriving. At this time, the principal sources of farm income were livestock and hay. During peak season, around 4,000 hay bales were shipped daily to northern points by rail. Grand Prairie hay was highly sought after in markets like Chicago. (Courtesy of Kay Tindall Trice.)

Prairie Hay, Ready for Shipment, Stuttgart, Ark.                    1052734

The first major cash crop in the Stuttgart area was hay cut from the fertile Grand Prairie soil. This postcard scene from around 1900 depicts wagonloads of hay heading up College Street to the Cotton Belt Railroad depot. The large building housed the Williamson Furniture Factory. Around 1909, the Stuttgart Rice Milling Company converted this structure for use as its second mill. (MAGP.)

Williamson Novelty Woodworks was a very early Stuttgart business. Shown here in the 1880s–1890s, the company was later known as Williamson Furniture Factory. The building would later be acquired and remodeled by the Stuttgart Rice Mill Company when it became necessary for the firm to increase milling capacity. (AC/SPL.)

This photograph of a team of oxen pulling a wagon in Stuttgart's Main Street is dated October 5, 1896, and possibly marks a family's arrival in the town. The view is toward the west side of Main Street near Fourth Street. The photograph is also marked "Southern emigration." (Courtesy of Kay Tindall Trice.)

H.E. Rhodes Concrete Works was vital to the construction of many of the town's early homes and businesses. The plant was located on the southeast corner of Leslie and Cleveland Streets. Pictured, from left to right, are H.E. Rhodes, Jacob Showalter, Herman Martin, five unidentified, Arthur Rhodes (smaller boy), and unidentified. (MAGP.)

Stuttgart Transfer Service operated a fleet of carriages and drayage equipment around 1900. Its customers included railroad passengers needing a ride to or from town, local businesses sending and receiving freight or express shipments, and citizens wanting a ride by taxi to another location around town. The service also offered horses and mules for sale. (MAGP.)

14

Early Stuttgart promoter Philip Reinsch is shown with Signal Belle, his favorite riding horse, on Main Street in this undated photograph. Reinsch was instrumental in the early development of the town. He owned the Stuttgart Driving Park (racetrack), which was near the northeast corner of Twenty-Second and Main Streets. (AC/SPL.)

Joe Bush, the first black citizen of Stuttgart, was brought from Lexington, Kentucky, in the late 1880s by Philip Reinsch to train his horses for harness racing. Bush is shown here with Cecil Girl and a racing sulky (cart). This horse was described as "sound and well-mannered and a trotter." Bush became an early Stuttgart property owner. (AC/SPL.)

A.H. Soekland, Ed Hall, and A.D. Swan incorporated Stuttgart Electric Light and Water Plant in 1888. Charles Williamson acquired it in 1897. Prominent early businesswoman Anna B. Stoops owned the facility from 1904 to 1916. This 1890s view, looking west along Sixth Street, shows the original First Christian Church building near Sixth and Main Streets. (Courtesy of the Arkansas History Commission.)

Simmermacher Saloon is pictured here around 1888. The men are, from left to right, unidentified, John Woerner, George Rhodes, and John Simmermacher. Early Stuttgart promotional material typically asserted that there were no saloons in the town; however, this photograph proves there was at least one. (Courtesy of the Arkansas History Commission.)

16

Claude and Virginia Hill Van Duyn are pictured with their daughter in this undated image. Van Duyn, along with his brother Glenn and their father, John, operated the Central Livery Stable on the northwest corner of Fourth and College Streets in the 1900s–1910s. (Courtesy of the *Stuttgart Daily Leader*.)

This well-dressed couple is enjoying a ride heading south past Second and Main Streets around 1910. The Dellmon Tin Shop is visible in the background, along with the taller rice mills at left and at far right. Second Street was known as Union Avenue in the early days and had quite a number of commercial structures at one time. (Courtesy of Kay Tindall Trice.)

RES. OF L.H. MORPHEW, M.D.
STUTTGART, ARK.
SEP. 25-09

The original part of this home was built around 1885 by early Stuttgart physician Dr. Veasey. After his death, Dr. Leander H. Morphew bought the residence and enlarged it. The house still stands at the southwest corner of Fourth and Maple Streets. Dr. Morphew operated a Rexall pharmacy for many years. (AC/SPL.)

Dr. Leander H. Morphew, one of Stuttgart's earliest and most popular doctors, moved to the young town in 1885 from Fairmount, a small community to the north. Dr. Morphew was one of the signers of the petition to incorporate Stuttgart, and the Rexall drugstore bore his name until the late 1950s. (AC/SPL.)

HOME OF W. M. PRICE, STUTTGART, ARK.

The W.M. "Mack" Price home at the northeast corner of Second and Anna Streets was for many years one of the showplaces of Stuttgart, even playing host to governors. Price figured prominently in the town's early growth. Built around 1900, the home later served as the Stuttgart Country Club until the late 1960s. (Courtesy of the Arkansas History Commission.)

This image of Hereford calves belonging to early Stuttgart promoter Philip Reinsch appeared in school geography books in the early 1900s. The scene was also used on postcards that read, "A Royal Flush—A Product of Grand Prairie, Stuttgart, Ark." The area was once known for its livestock and haying enterprises. (MAGP.)

Business Street Scene, Stuttgart, Ark.

In this view looking north at the intersection of Fourth and Main Streets, the office of early Stuttgart realtor and promoter Olaf H. Kyster can be seen. Today, the edifice is known as the Denman Building. The three-story bank building now next door on the corner had not yet been constructed, dating this postcard image to before 1910. (Courtesy of the Butler Center for Arkansas Studies.)

Main Street, looking South, Stuttgart, Ark.

This 1900s view of Main Street, looking south from Second Street, shows a growing town. Two of Stuttgart's prominent land offices, those of Elliott Tallman and D.C. Adams, can be seen at left. These and other realtors arranged excursions on the St. Louis Southwestern (nicknamed "the Cotton Belt") Railroad from northern points on the first and third Tuesdays of each month in the 1900–1910 period, greatly increasing area population. (MAGP.)

Frank and Naomi Glenn pose on horseback by their home at 501 East Sixth Street in the early 1900s. The couple arrived from Missouri in 1904 following his graduation from medical school. Dr. Glenn practiced as an osteopath until 1931. Their sons Howard and Harold Glenn were also Stuttgart osteopaths. Naomi Glenn's father, Jacob Showalter, built this home in 1904, and it still stands today. (Author's collection.)

Located at Eleventh and Lowe Streets and still standing today, this home was built by Augustus and Mary Alice Tindall, who moved to Stuttgart from Piper City, Illinois, in the very early 1900s. This was the time that Grand Prairie lands were being advertised and sold to people living in the Midwest. The Tindalls were parents of five children, including Verne and Art Tindall. (Courtesy of Kay Tindall Trice.)

Early Stuttgart entrepreneur Homer E. Rhodes was a dealer for the Parlin & Orendorff Plow Company of Illinois, later a part of International Harvester. Its dependable line of implements served the region's hay and rice farmers well. The Rhodes family would be known for many successful Stuttgart enterprises over the years. (MAGP.)

Naomi (Showalter) Glenn stands before her home on the southeast corner of Ninth Street and Grand Avenue. The Frank H. Glenn family occupied this house for a time in the early 1900s. Later, Dr. M.C. John built the brick home still standing on this lot. The home visible in the right background still stands on Leslie Street. (Author's collection.)

22

This photograph of the west side of Main Street just north of Third Street was taken around 1910. The building at left, now heavily altered, is the oldest (1889) building on Main Street. It is occupied today by Wilkerson Jewelers. The two young girls are Ledia (left) and Revillo Ware, who lived in the house standing on the southeast corner of Tenth and Leslie Streets. (AC/SPL.)

The Williams Variety Store on the west side of Main Street between Third and Fourth Streets was one of the town's early dime stores. Identified are, from left to right, (left side) Mrs. Robert Woolfolk and Mr. and Mrs. Tom Williams; (at center) Mrs. Kissack, Irene Payne Krummen, and Nellie Collins Newbold; (right side) Ethel Mallory Walton, Olga Buerkle Jensen, and Katye Wessels Mommsen. The others pictured in the background are unidentified. (AC/SPL.)

Looking north along Main Street from near Third Street, this view from around 1910 depicts Stuttgart at a time when the horseless carriage was becoming the transportation of choice. At left, the balconied Price Hotel served as the town's most prestigious accommodation. Hotel owner W.M. "Mack" Price, also a realtor and promoter, was responsible for enticing many new settlers to the area. (AC/SPL.)

The Bank of Commerce opened in 1904 near the southeast corner of Third and Main Streets. From left to right are Clara McPherson Wofford, unidentified, Ray Underwood, Clement J. Brain, and Sidney Brain. The bank was closed in 1914. Many banking institutions would come and go over the years in small towns like Stuttgart. (AC/SPL.)

One of Stuttgart's earliest automobile dealers, shown around 1912, was this firm owned by Louis H. Thielman. It was located on the north side of Second Street east of Leslie Street, on the site later occupied by the Fairbanks-Morse plant. Several makes of autos are already present in the town at this early date. (AC/SPL.)

Minnie Pierron's Millinery Shop on the east side of the 400 block of Main Street is shown here around 1910; it is full of customers selecting their fine Easter hats. Pictured, from left to right, are Mathilda (Mrs. Philip) Scheiderer, Esther Scroggins Stuckey, Bertha Moritz, owner Minnie (Mrs. Edward) Pierron, hat trimmer Clara Cassidy, and unidentified. (MAGP.)

This photograph from around 1910 depicts a busy day along the west side of Main Street between Fourth and Sixth Streets. Helm Furniture Company occupied part of the H.E. Rhodes Concrete Building, where the BancorpSouth parking lot is now located. They are obviously doing a lot of office business on this day. In the center, a Singer sewing machine demonstration is taking place, along with a free machine promotion. In 1910, the Comet Theatre, named after the appearance

A BUSY DAY
STUTTGART ARK

of Halley's comet, opened in the Rhodes Building. The smaller brick building at left housed Dr. Sillin's office around this time. Dr. H.V. Glenn's osteopathic practice occupied it from the 1940s to the 1960s. It was razed in 1965 and replaced by the current building at 424 South Main Street. To the right of Helm Furniture are Story's Variety Store and the City Hotel. (AC/SPL.)

The Cotton Belt Railroad began service from St. Louis to Texas through Stuttgart in 1883. For many years, a frame depot, located between College Street and Grand Avenue south of the track, served the town. In 1910, the railroad built a new Mission Revival–style brick depot on the same site. This photograph is believed to have been taken shortly after the new station's opening. The only person identified is Dr. Frank H. Glenn, standing on the rail. The article "New Station Will Be a Dandy One," in the May 23, 1910, *Stuttgart Arkansawyer*, describes the soon-to-be opened station as follows: "Two stories in height, 326 feet long and 35 feet wide. The first floor will consist of two waiting rooms with ticket offices in the center. The west portion of the building will be used for freight. The second story will be given over to offices. The building will be of St. Louis pressed brick with tiled roof and floors. The trimmings are to be of cut-stone terracotta. The building will be handsomely finished inside, with modern plumbing, electric lights, and every other convenience possible to put in." (Author's collection.)

This undated view of the interior of the Cotton Belt Railroad's Stuttgart depot depicts the agent's office with the telegrapher's station by the bay window at right. A careful look at the incoming message "sounder" box will reveal a tobacco can wedged in the apparatus. This improvisation magnified the sound for the telegrapher, who often had other noises such as passing trains to contend with. (MAGP.)

Charley Burns (left) shows off his Mitchell automobile to John Wiley around 1910. Behind them is the Illinois House Hotel, which welcomed visitors from that area of the Midwest arriving in response to Stuttgart's early real estate promoters. Many of the city's present families descend from these pioneers. The hotel was located across from the Cotton Belt Railroad depot on the northeast corner of Grand Avenue and Harrison Street. (AC/SPL.)

Stuttgart has had many newspapers over the years. In the early days, there were as many as five at a time, including a German-language newspaper. W.L. "Pink" Kennedy was one of the city's most beloved journalists. One of his printing offices is pictured here in 1911, with, from left to right, Anna Martin, unidentified, Pink Kennedy, and Emma Martin. (AC/SPL.)

The *Stuttgart Free Press* had offices on East Fourth Street between Main and College Streets, on the site later occupied by the Food Bank. Shown in this undated photograph are, from left to right, two unidentified people, Anna Martin, Emma Martin (seated), and W.C. Moore. The Martins worked in most of the early newspaper offices in town. (Courtesy of the *Stuttgart Daily Leader*.)

Harper-Croom Dry Goods was located at 303 South Main Street. The firm carried a full range of consumer goods not offered by hardware or grocery stores, including fabrics, home furnishings, ready-to-wear clothing, shoes, and sundries. Present in this 1919 photograph are, from left to right, Samuel Harper, Mabel Thomas, and Mrs. Woersing. (MAGP.)

Wakefield and Virgil Menees sold fine gents' furnishings in the 1910s–1920s at their store on the southeast corner of Fourth and Main Streets. The three-story building was first called the Johnson Building and was later known as the Exchange Building after a tenant bank. Signs in the window announce "We Don't Credit" as well as "Style Headquarters where Society Brand Clothes are Sold." (Courtesy of the Butler Center for Arkansas Studies.)

The Williamson family home, pictured here in 1908, stood at Sixth and College Streets. This house was destroyed by a December 1910 fire. Early Stuttgart businessman Charles Williamson owned a large furniture factory and woodworks, as well as the town's electric and water plant located on East Sixth Street. (AC/SPL.)

This photograph of Stuttgart's Main Street, taken from Fourth Street with a view looking north, indicates that by this time the automobile had all but replaced the horse and buggy on the Grand Prairie. One obvious exception was the carriage driven by prominent businessman Joseph I. Porter. He and his brother James W. Porter owned lumberyards in Stuttgart and DeWitt, respectively. (Courtesy of the Arkansas History Commission.)

This photograph from Stuttgart High School's top floor in the 1910s provides a view to the northeast from Seventh and Lowe Streets. Visible in the background are the rice mills and steeples of the Catholic, Emanuel Lutheran, Methodist (South), and Christian churches, as well as the cupola of the frame school building. (Courtesy of Kay Tindall Trice.)

From shortly after Stuttgart was founded until the 1920s, there were regular unsuccessful attempts to drill for oil in the area. Several of the larger ventures took place after World War I. Many citizens lost their money waiting for the gusher that never came. J.E. Balle's well was located north of the city. (AC/SPL.)

A World War I troop train leaves Stuttgart on the England branch of the Cotton Belt Railroad in September 1917, bound for Camp Pike in North Little Rock. The passenger cars are leaning noticeably due to the soldiers hanging out of the windows to greet the crowd. The view below was taken on the same day as the troop train departure. Stuttgart Ice Cream and Bottling Company is visible on Grand Avenue. The bottling plant building stood directly south of the depot and also housed a café. In the background is one of the Stuttgart Rice Mill Company's facilities. (Both, author's collection.)

Leonard Krumpen operated a machine shop specializing in equipment for the rice industry. His original shop was in the 100 block of South College Street. Later, he built this structure located on the west side of College Street just north of the railroad tracks. Eddie Gollon Automotive Repair later occupied the building for many years. (Courtesy of the *Stuttgart Daily Leader*.)

This interior view of Krumpen Machine Shop shows a busy firm engaged in fabricating equipment used in farming and local industry. Owner Leonard Krumpen is seen on the stool, and machinist L.H. Brown is second from left. Others are unidentified. With all the unguarded belts running in a shop such as this, safety must have been a constant concern. (MAGP.)

Fairbanks-Morse Company opened a new office in this building of ornamental concrete block construction around 1920. It sold rice field irrigation and pumping equipment. Names written next to the automobiles are, from left to right, Nash, Ford, Ford, Ford, ?, Eppley, Smith, Roberts, Williams, Hahn, Redken, Witte, Sherwood, Young, and Ham. Crow-Burlingame Company later occupied this building for many years until the 2000s. (AC/SPL.)

Conrey and Ham Machinery Company supplied many of the items needed by rice growers and affiliated companies. The firm's Stuttgart branch operated at this location on the southeast corner of First and Main Streets. Other outlets were in DeWitt and Carlisle. Later, Duckett Pontiac Company occupied this building. (AC/SPL.)

This aerial photograph of Stuttgart was taken in the mid-1920s. Arkmo Lumber Company is the larger building in the foreground, near the Second Street and Grand Avenue intersection. This view shows that the East Second Street corridor was well occupied with commercial buildings in those days. Main Street had mostly acquired what would become its modern appearance by this time. (Courtesy of the Arkansas History Commission.)

The Riceland Hotel, opened in 1923 on the southwest corner of Third and Main Streets, featured a separate ground-floor section on the front, originally occupied by the Exchange Bank and later by the Sterling Variety Store. The hotel advertised itself as the "Palace of the Rice Belt." During duck hunting seasons, the Riceland hosted many celebrities. It was closed in 1970. (Courtesy of the Arkansas History Commission.)

Standard Oil of Louisiana operated a filling station at the southwest corner of Sixth and Main Streets. This mid-1920s view shows the station after the brand name was changed from Stanocola. Later, the subsidiary was absorbed into its corporate parent Standard Oil (Esso), which built a newer station on the site. First Christian Church is visible behind the station, before its move to a new building at Tenth and Main Streets. (MAGP.)

The 555 Shell service station crew poses for the camera at the business on the southwest corner of Fourth and College Streets. The station was also a Firestone dealership for many years. At the time of this photograph, a gallon of Silver Shell gasoline was selling for 8.5¢ with 7.5¢ tax added. Spark plugs were cleaned for a nickel. 555 Shell gave Eagle trading stamps for purchases. (MAGP.)

The 1927 gathering pictured here is believed to be related to the great flood of that year. Possibly, the group is looking into relief benefits. The scene is on the southeast corner of Fourth and Main Streets. Arkansas Rice Growers Cooperative had offices in the three-story corner building. Signs for B.L. Williams Music and Downing Photography Studio can been seen farther along the street. (Courtesy of University of Arkansas at Little Rock, Arkansas Studies Institute.)

A considerable crowd has gathered around the large Christmas tree at Third and Main Streets in this c. 1927 photograph. Several persons can be seen on an adjacent rooftop. Businesses visible in this scene include the F.E. Erstine Maxwell automobile dealership, Stuttgart Hardware, and the City Café. (Courtesy of Myrtle Sampson Welch.)

Dr. John B. Bryant served Stuttgart's black community for many years beginning in 1913, after graduation from Meharry Medical College. His office was at 407 North Maple Street. Dr. Bryant established a teen center for youth activities and was instrumental in obtaining funding for a new school. He was recognized with a new city park named in his honor in 1953. Dr. Bryant died in the late 1950s. (Courtesy of Mrs. B.T. Releford.)

Hartz-Thorell Supply Company was located on the southwest corner of Second and College Streets. The firm was a dealer for International Harvester farm machinery, serving area rice farmers. This late-1920s picture shows, from left to right, two unidentified people, Francis Strabala, Sallie Stillwell, unidentified, Alfred R. Thorell, George Hartz, and Jacob Hartz. In later years, the business would be known as A.R. Thorell Supply Company. (MAGP.)

Stuttgart aviator Garland "Buddy" Rhodes poses with his Command-Aire Challenger in the 1930s. He gained fame as a stuntman and aerial acrobat. Rhodes jumped out of an airplane at 19,500 feet over Little Rock Airport on March 15, 1931, setting a record for the longest delayed parachute jump in history. His father and brother built an airplane in 1915, and it is believed to have been the first one built in Arkansas. (MAGP.)

Townsend Lumber Company's mill and yard are shown in this undated photograph. The firm, owned by Mark Townsend, operated for many years at this location north of the Cotton Belt Railroad tracks between Leslie and Anna Streets. Two Esso gasoline pumps are visible in front of the office—one is of the older glass-cylinder variety. (MAGP.)

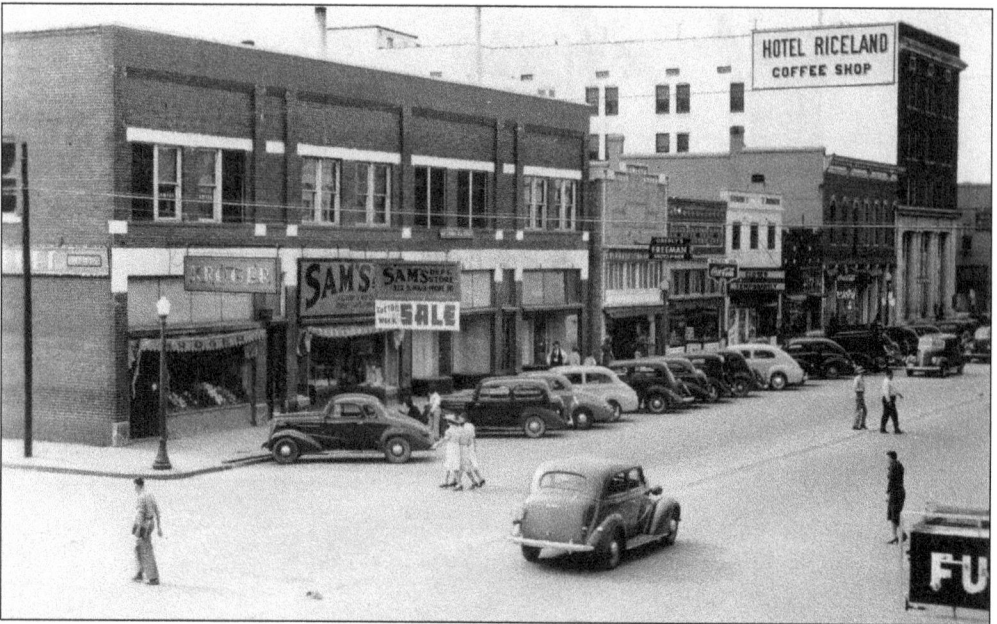

The intersection of Fourth and Main Streets, in this view looking northwest, was photographed from the three-story bank building that still stands across the street. Businesses visible are Kroger Grocery, Sam's Department Store, Oberly's Shoes, Wilcox Grocery, Strand Theater, Watkins Café, and the Riceland Hotel. This glimpse at a typically busy afternoon in the downtown area dates to around 1940. (AC/SPL.)

Boone Hayes (center) poses with employees in front of his plumbing and heating business. The shop was located at 408 South Main Street, where Bancorp South now stands. The photograph dates to a time when this block still had several wooden buildings left over from the early 20th century. (MAGP.)

The Stuttgart & Rice Belt Railroad built a line from Mesa, on the Rock Island's main line near DeValls Bluff, to Stuttgart in 1911. The Rock Island Railroad acquired the line in 1913 to gain access to the lucrative rice industry revenue around Stuttgart. The attractive depot pictured here was built on the north side of First Street near College Street. At the peak of passenger service in the 1920s, Rock Island usually scheduled a mixed train on the branch, hauling freight cars as well as either a passenger coach or caboose with seating. In this way, riders could connect to main line trains bound for Memphis, Little Rock, Oklahoma, and points west. The branch was freight-only after the 1930s. The depot was demolished around the 1940s; however, a near-identical twin of the station's passenger portion remains standing at Hazen. The Rock Island's Stuttgart branch operated until 1980, when the railroad entered bankruptcy, and was removed in 1982. (AC/SPL.)

The Kroger Grocery Company's store was originally on the northwest corner of Fourth and Main Streets. Notable in this interior view from 1935 are the turnstile marked "This Way In," the baskets provided for shoppers, and the displays of Alco Lard and Ferry Seeds. The only person identified is James G. Allen, third from left. Kroger later occupied two other locations along South Main Street. (MAGP.)

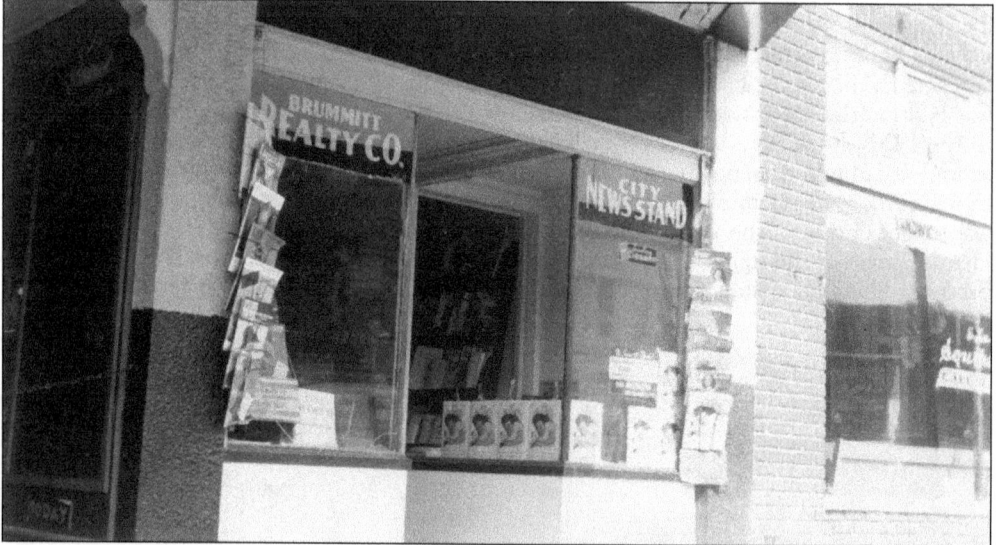

Brummitt Realty and City Newsstand, located at 310 South Main Street, were owned and operated by Eva Dinwiddie Brummitt, mother of Willie (Mrs. Verne) Tindall and Mrs. Jack Wright. She moved to Stuttgart with her husband from McKenzie, Tennessee, in 1904. Eva Brummitt was one of the first lady entrepreneurs in Stuttgart. She also owned and managed an apartment house on Lowe Street across from Stuttgart High School. (Courtesy of Kay Tindall Trice.)

This c. 1940 view, looking southeast from the Lion Oil Company service station's forecourt at Sixth and Main Streets, shows its brand of "Knix Knox" gasoline selling for 16¢ per gallon. Across Main Street on the left, the Horst Goodyear/Conoco station is matching Lion's price. The brick buildings across the street house the Daniel Harder American Legion Post No. 48 (left) and Arkansas Power and Light Company. The small addition on the side of the latter structure was originally built to house an ice plant. The sign of Standard Oil's Esso station can be seen on right. That station stood across Sixth Street from Lion Oil. Today, all that remains of this nostalgic scene is the frame house with the dormer window, visible to the right of the utility company's offices. (Courtesy of the *Stuttgart Daily Leader*.)

The US Army Air Forces opened the Stuttgart Army Airfield as a pilot training base in late 1942, six miles north of the city on 2,681 acres. The air base consisted of four 5,000-foot runways and facilities for 6,000 personnel. Officials decided on Stuttgart because the prairie environment was perfect for airfield operations, with little clearing necessary and firm hardpan soil for runways. The school was originally an advanced twin-engine facility and was activated as such in August 1942. In October 1942, glider classes were transferred to Stuttgart so that students could take advantage of the year-round flying conditions and obstruction-free prairie. Pilots trained on the Waco CG-4A Hadrian glider until May 1943. From then until January 1945, the airfield was again used for twin-engine training. After the deactivation of the base in 1945, the War Assets Administration took over the field in 1946. In 1949, the land was transferred to the city for use as a municipal airport. Today, it is one of the busiest airports in Arkansas. (Air Force Heritage Research Agency.)

# Two

# SCHOOL, CHURCH, AND SOCIAL LIFE

This Mitchell automobile was owned by Philip Reinsch, but as with many early car owners, he hired someone to drive it. Pictured are, from left to right, (front) August Hoevels, Hugo Reinsch, and Philip Reinsch; (back) Esther Hoevels (on running board), Erna Hoevels, Louisa Hoevels, and Christina Reinsch, almost hidden behind Hoevels. (AC/SPL.)

Stuttgart's first school was built around 1882 near the southwest corner of Fourth and Main Streets. The austere structure cost $200 to build. Eliza Starkey (far right in back row) was the teacher at the time of this c. 1887 photograph. This one-room school was used until the fall of 1889, when a new four-room school was built at Fourth and Leslie Streets. The house in background was Joseph I. Porter's home at Fourth and Maple Streets. Identified in the picture are, alphabetically, Lillie Barricklow, Ollie Deets, Alf Harper, Cardie Harper, Ollie Harper, Sam Harper, Norma Heinmiller, Rose Heinmiller, Floyd Homer, Arnold Kleiner, Roy Kleiner, Will Kleiner, Lizzie Leker, Doug Mahle, Webster Mahle, Mollie McFall, Dessie Parker, Clyde Pettit, Hallie Redd, Mattie Rhodes, John Ryan, Dennis Ryan, Mary Ryan, Nellie Ryan, Myrtie Siefield, teacher Eliza Starkey. (AC/SPL.)

Stuttgart's second school, built 1889, faced south on Fourth Street west of Leslie Street, at today's First United Methodist Church location. It was the only public school until 1912, when a new brick school opened at Ninth and Lowe Streets. It served as the county courthouse until the present one was built in 1928. The Julia Shannon Grade School was then built on this site. Taken at the school in 1894, the photograph below is the earliest dated image of the town's high school students. The only students identified are, alphabetically, Dolorious Barnes, Arnold Kleiner, Doug Mahle, Ethel Moran, and Mark Underwood. (Both, courtesy of the Arkansas History Commission.)

During its time as Stuttgart College, and later Training School, the institution educated many of the town's early citizens and leaders. Students and teachers at the school around 1909 are, from left to right, (first row) unidentified, Charles Chaney, two unidentified, Arthur Pettit, two unidentified, and Myron Williams; (second row) Gladys Hegner, Joanna Porter, Edna Holdridge, Harvey Pace, John Hegner, Walter Mobley, and teacher Miss Varney; (third row) principal C. O'Rear, Florence Sumner, unidentified, Evelyn Clark, Willie Brummitt, Mattie Simmermacher, Verna Huffman, John Holdridge, Wesley Clark, and teacher Miss Bodenhamer; (fourth row) Josie Satchfield, Belle McFall, two unidentified, Bertha Griffin, Blanche Leighton, Alice Bradford, Myrtle Hostetter, Edith Leighton, Willie Lee Spiller, and Fred Wilcox; (fifth row) Jennie Hostetter, teacher John G. Rossman, teacher Ralph Standley, Earl Moorhead, Richard Miller, Roy Hawley, and Floyd Denman; (sixth row) Robert Moorhead, William Adams, Duncan Moore, Kenneth Yoder, Ben Ware, Arch Vickers, unidentified, and Lloyd Moorhead. (AC/SPL.)

Prominent early educator Julia Shannon moved to Stuttgart from Paris, Kentucky, and beginning in 1892, she taught school for the next 47 years. She continued her education by taking graduate course work from Columbia University, the University of Colorado, and the University of California, Berkeley. Julia Shannon's long service to Stuttgart education was recognized by the naming of an elementary school for her. (AC/SPL.)

Stuttgart Training School stood at the south end of College Street on Fifteenth Street. It opened as Stuttgart College around 1890, associated with the Methodist and later Presbyterian Church. In 1906, it was reacquired by the Methodist Church and operated as a preparatory school. Many of Stuttgart's successful early citizens were trained in the arts and sciences at this facility. The school closed around World War I. (MAGP.)

The Baptist railroad chapel car *Evangel* is shown at Stuttgart in May 1897 with a sizable local crowd. Rev. and Mrs. John S. Thomas were assigned to the car and lived on board in Pullman-style accommodations. The car included a chapel and organ in addition to the living quarters. *Evangel* was one of 13 chapel cars operated on railroads from 1890 to 1946 by the Catholic, Episcopal, and Baptist denominations. The cars served as churches on wheels, offering Christian services and education. They were especially useful early on as western lands were settled. Many churches and Sunday schools were started as a result of the chapel cars, and Bibles and other religious materials were distributed in many languages. Railroad workers were ministered to during westward expansion. *Evangel*, dedicated in 1891 and operated until 1924, was the first Baptist chapel car. It traveled Southern states from 1894 to 1901 and made many Arkansas visits. *Evangel* was last stationed at Rawlins, Wyoming. In 1924, it became a temporary meeting place for local Baptists. When the congregation erected a church, *Evangel* was incorporated into the building, where it remains today. (MAGP.)

Some of Stuttgart's social leaders pose for a picture around 1905. The ladies are (front) Annie Underwood Morphew; (second row) Julia Shannon and Dena Soekland Hurd; (third row) Dora Strong White and Mabel Price Gunn. Hurd married a railroad official and, upon a return visit to Stuttgart, had her own private railcar. (AC/SPL.)

The inscription on the reverse of this photograph reads, "Spiller and some neighborhood kids, first Rice Carnival, 1909." Note the displays of rice placed around the carriage and fine crepe decorations on the wheels. Families dressed up their vehicles and wore their Sunday best in hopes of winning one of the prizes. (AC/SPL.)

Some of the students at Stuttgart School on Fourth Street pose for the camera in 1906. The only persons identified are, alphabetically, teacher Ida (Mrs. Louis) Buerkle, Wilda Carter, Flora Conn, Hazel Davis, Lucille Morphew, Miriam Stillwell, Verne Tindall, and Clara Wheeler. The building would serve as a school until 1912. (AC/SPL.)

The 1906 confirmation class of Emanuel Lutheran Church proudly poses for the camera. Pictured are, from left to right, (first row) Henry Stutzenbaker, Adolph Wessels, Rev. C.H. Hauser, Wilhelm Lucus, and Herbert Weber; (second row) Maria Harer, Sophie Harer, Herman Duensing, Albert Lammers, August Young, Fritz Young, and Emma Mertens; (third row) Johannah Mauer, Christine Dreher, Martha Reich, and Emma Eifling. (Courtesy of Emanuel Lutheran Church.)

54

Stuttgart High School opened in 1912 to replace the overcrowded public school at Fourth and Leslie Streets. It served all grades in the white school system until 1928. The handsome building at Ninth and Lowe Streets graduated 55 classes of area students. It was torn down in early 1968, after being replaced by a new high school campus on the south edge of the city. (AC/SPL.)

Chautauqua was a highly popular adult education movement in the late 1800s and early 1900s. Named after a lake in Upstate New York where the first meeting was held, Chautauqua assemblies expanded and spread throughout rural America. The Stuttgart Chautauqua brought entertainment and culture for the whole community, with speakers, teachers, musicians, entertainers, preachers, and specialists of the day. (AC/SPL.)

The 1918 graduating class of Stuttgart High School poses with a teacher. Pictured are, from left to right, (first row) Louise Tallman, Esther Gettle, Freddie Mattmiller, Edna Meyers, Lula Waggoner, Mable Trimble, Pauline Buerkle, Olga Reinsch, Helena Scheeler, Revillo Ware, and Alice Beeble; (second row) Mildred Barnes, Ruby Thomason, Esther Weidner, Maylene Rowland, Herbert Pierron, Grant Williams, Joseph Peltier, Adolph Sickel, Gerda Kyster, Martha Scheeler, and Paul Hollingshead; (third row) Frank Martin, Hubert Doty, Monroe Procop, Howard Morphew, Prof. John G. Rossman, Willis O'Dell, Cyrus King, Harold Glenn, and Clarence Walker. Below, the 1918 track team and coach take time off for a group portrait. Pictured are, from left to right, Herbert Pierron, Johnny Woerner, Frank Martin, Hubert Doty, Arthur Seidenschwarz, Carroll Robnolt, Harold Glenn, Cyrus King, James Tallman, and coach Ralph Hunt. (Both, author's collection.)

St. John's Lutheran Church was originally built at Lone Tree Cemetery in 1882. The frame building was moved to Fourth and College Streets in 1885, becoming the first church within the city limits. In 1914, the congregation built this brick church at the same location. It was replaced by a third building in 1949 on the same block. (MAGP.)

In this view looking north from the corner of Fourth and Main Streets, the camera captured a Fourth of July parade in 1914 or 1915. The Hurd-Ahlfeldt Grocery and Williams Bargain Store are visible at left in the Pettit Building. The columned Price Hotel can be seen at the other end of the block. (MAGP.)

The Delmonico Café was considered the finest place to eat in Stuttgart in its time. The eatery, operated by J.J. Woolfolk and Jack Elliott, was located in the Metropolitan Hotel on the west side of Main Street, south of Third Street. After the Metropolitan relocated around the corner to West Third Street, the Price Hotel occupied the building and was Stuttgart's nicest lodging accommodation. (AC/SPL.)

This group is headed to an early Rice Carnival in a decorated automobile. From left to right are (front seat) the unidentified driver and Philip Reinsch; (backseat) Christina Reinsch and Anna B. Stoops. The latter was a prominent businesswoman, civic leader, and one of the originators of the Rice Carnival. The photograph was taken in front of the Reinsch home at Third and College Streets. (AC/SPL.)

First Baptist Church. Stuttgart, Ark.

First Baptist Church's second building was constructed on the southeast corner of Third Street and Grand Avenue in 1916 by E.W. McCollum. The church was destroyed by fire in January 1920. A new building was erected on the same site, and would serve the congregation until the 1960s. (Author's collection.)

The Methodist Episcopal Church South was located on the northeast corner of Fourth Street and Grand Avenue. The congregation, now known as First United Methodist Church, is still located on the same block. Stuttgart is unusual in that the city had both Northern and Southern Methodist congregations dating from its early days. (Courtesy of Kay Tindall Trice.)

This photograph of Pontiac School around 1922 is a rare look inside a country schoolhouse in the Stuttgart area. From left to right are (first row) Frances Heien, Dorothy Ross, Hazel Thompson, and Velma Harris; (second row) Rachel Thompson, Helen Heien, and Dorothy Beck; (third row, standing) Harold Shirkey, Orin Shirkey, Lindsey Burnett, Verne Scroggins, Glenn Boyce, and Marvin Scroggins. The teacher is Nancy Long. (AC/SPL.)

The Stuttgart Ad Club Band is shown here in 1923 dressed in military-style uniforms. From left to right are (first row) ? Derocher, K.D. Shupe, W.D. Petty, Jack Dillon, Harry Baker, Cleve Harris, and Si King; (second row) Herman Woerner, Martin Koch, Bill Kornbaum, Fred Balmer, and unidentified; (third row) Herman Packebush, Cliff Shurtz, Fred Wessels, and Bill Morrel. (AC/SPL.)

These lively early-1920s Stuttgart High School ladies are known as the "Ukulele Girls." The girls are, from left to right, (first row) Joy Oaksmith, Margaret Horst, and Ruby Taylor; (second row) Louise Buerkle, Margaret McGahhey, Oweta Kesterson, Louise John, Margaret Shriver, Blanche Maners, Hazel Maners, Karen Kyster, and Julia Durr. (AC/SPL.)

A good example of an early Rice Carnival float is this one by Stuttgart realtor and promoter Ray O. Burks. It represents a home flanked by the bountiful harvest of the Grand Prairie. The roof is covered with fruits, vegetables, and rice shocks, while corn and rice adorn the sides. (Courtesy of the Butler Center for Arkansas Studies.)

Built as the local lodge of the Benevolent and Protective Order of Elks, this building also hosted the Masonic Lodge as well as Turpin Funeral Home over the years. The building at the northwest corner of Fourth and College Streets later served as an annex to the Arkansas County Courthouse before being destroyed by fire in 2014. (MAGP.)

This postcard view of the 1923 Rice Carnival is set in the 300 block of Main Street looking north. In the middle of the street is an exhibition tent sponsored by St. Albans Episcopal Church. Stuttgart held the carnival most years from 1909 until the advent of the National Duck Calling Contest in 1936. (Author's collection.)

Looking north from Third and Main Streets, this view of an early Rice Carnival parade features an entry from Starley White's Machine Works. The carnival was apparently not held every year in the early days. It originated in 1909 shortly after the founding of the rice mills, to promote the industry and generate civic pride. (MAGP.)

The 1924 Rice Carnival was well attended, as this view from above Morphew Rexall Drugs attests. The pharmacy adjacent to Rexall was Crowe Drug Company. City Café's sign is visible farther up the east side of Main Street. All were longtime Stuttgart businesses. On the west side, the Peoples Store is seen on the Third Street corner. The Riceland Hotel, far left, had only been open about a year. (MAGP.)

The candidates for Rice Carnival queen are ready to join the parade on their fancy float in this undated photograph. In this view looking north from Second and College Streets, Moll Motor Company and the City Hotel are visible. Harold "Pete" Moll and family operated several successful businesses in Stuttgart over the years. (MAGP.)

An early Rice Carnival provides the backdrop for a tightrope walker to demonstrate his skill above the crowded intersection of Third and Main Streets in Stuttgart. Visible in this northeast view are Erstine Hardware and First National Bank (across Third Street) and Conn and Underwood Hardware at far right. (MAGP.)

Mack's Café was originally located on the southwest corner of Fourth and Main Streets. Identified in this 1928 photograph are (left) Mack McCallister and (third from left) Roman Selig. The eatery was later at First and Main Streets on the west side. Selig would later operate the Selig Sandwich Shop at 210 South Main Street. (MAGP.)

The Stuttgart Citizens Band poses for the camera next to the Rock Island depot at First and College Streets. The only member identified is (second row, sixth from left) Harry Edward Baker, who played in several military and community bands. Cities sponsored such bands, which consisted mainly of amateur musicians and performed at holiday and patriotic events. (MAGP.)

James Barrett constructed First Christian Church's current building in 1928 at Tenth and Main Streets on the northeast corner. One of the earliest congregations in Stuttgart, it originally met on the southwest corner of Sixth and Main Streets. Around 1915, a larger frame church was acquired or built on the lot where the *Stuttgart Daily Leader* office is today. (MAGP.)

The Julia Shannon Grade School faced east on Leslie Street, between Third and Fourth Streets. The school was built in 1928, replacing the 1889 frame building, which had once served grades one through twelve. It was torn down in the late 1960s upon the opening of the new Julia Shannon (now Park Avenue) Elementary School. (MAGP.)

Members of Stuttgart High School's successful 1929 football team and coaches pose for the camera. The Stuttgart Ricebirds were considered a football powerhouse in those days, and have generally had a winning program in the years before and since. Pictured, from left to right, are (first row) Charlie Hagaman, Louis Reinhart, Howard Hagaman, Mark Townsend, Wilmer Loveless, Delphied Brown, and George Reigler; (second row) Billy Roy, Cullen McVey, Bill Burnett, Allen Keith, Bud Nichols, and Frank Brummitt; (third row) Milton Gingerich, Porter John, Sidney Brain, Kermit Kerksieck, Arthur Bruce, Kenneth Oaksmith, and ? Foley; (fourth row) coach Buck Wells, Risdon Wood, and Leland Morgans. Coach Wells would later move on to Fort Smith where he was athletic director at a local school for over 30 years. A stadium was named in his honor. (AC/SPL.)

Members of the Stuttgart Garden Club are shown here around 1930. They are, from left to right, Mrs. H.C. Ogletree, Mrs. Gillespie, Mabel (Mrs. Jim) Drummond, Marie Selig, Maude Bethel Lewis, unidentified, Blanche (Mrs. Martin Sr.) Koch, Mrs. D.P. Oaksmith, Mrs. Jake Gartner, and Mrs. Lee. The refreshments on this day appear to be lemonade, tea, and coffee. (AC/SPL.)

John Cain Park was dedicated on July 4, 1938. It was named for a local farmer who died without heirs and left his estate to the City of Stuttgart "for the purpose of purchasing, equipping and beautifying a park as near to the center of population as possible to be convenient for children." The park featured the usual playground equipment, plus a swimming pool, tennis courts, and baseball stadium. (Author's collection.)

An early Stuttgart educator, Prof. L.D. Holman is pictured with his students in this undated image. He began teaching here in 1907, when the black school was at McKinley and Spring Streets, above the Masonic Hall. In the 1920s, the Rosenwald-funded Stuttgart School was built at 412 North Porter Street and was renamed for Holman in 1932. High school grades were added in 1938, and the first class graduated in 1942. Prof. Holman died around 1940. Holman School teachers Mrs. Winn (left) and Cleo Givens are pictured at right in 1948. (Above, courtesy of Mrs. B.T. Releford; right, courtesy of the *Stuttgart Daily Leader*.)

Rev. Adam Buerkle, Stuttgart's founder, established Emanuel Lutheran Church in 1879. Early services were held at his home northwest of Stuttgart. The first church building was erected in 1896 along North Buerkle Road and was moved to Third Street and Grand Avenue in 1902. A new brick church, pictured here, was dedicated on the same site in 1950. (Courtesy of Emanuel Lutheran Church.)

Shown here around the time of the 1949 dedication, St. John's Lutheran Church erected its current buildings on the northeast corner of Fifth and College Streets. The original parsonage, seen at right, fronted Fifth Street. St. John's was formed when several families left Emanuel Lutheran Church around 1882 and formed their own congregation, building a frame church at what became Lone Tree Cemetery. (MAGP.)

Buerkle Street Elementary School was opened in 1952 at Nineteenth and Buerkle Streets. Stuttgart was experiencing postwar population growth and needed more space for grade school children. At the time, the only elementary school for white children was Julia Shannon Grade School. Buerkle Street Elementary was later renamed for longtime school system leader James Gingerich and was torn down in 2009. (AC/SPL.)

Located on West Nineteenth Street, Stuttgart Junior High School was opened in 1957. It was later renamed Stuttgart Middle School and is now named for a longtime educator and school system leader, George Meekins. It seems the preferred mode of transportation among the teenagers in this era was the bicycle. (AC/SPL.)

This early afternoon baseball game took place at Harmon Field, part of the Stuttgart High School sports complex at the end of West Ninth Street. Adjacent were a football field with the same name and a track. On this day in the 1950s, the team is playing in front of a "full house." (AC/SPL.)

Esquire Grill, shown here in the 1940s, was a popular eatery on the west side of Main Street between Third and Fourth Streets. Operated by Jack and Ann Hefley, the café survived well into the period of business district decline brought on by the coming of mass retailers and fast-food outlets. (MAGP.)

Holman School, located on the west side of Buerkle Street between McKinley and Jefferson Streets, originally occupied a frame structure built around 1932. Named for early Stuttgart educator L.D. Holman, the facility graduated its first class in 1942. The graduates were Ellen Age, Willie Mae Jackson, Jesse Lamb, Robert Scroggins, Audrey Skinner, Albert Thompkins, and Savanna Carter Wright. Around 1950, this brick school was built on the same site to consolidate all grades of Stuttgart's black students. The last Holman class would graduate in 1970. The building now houses the Holman Heritage Community Center. Pictured at right around 1968 are two Holman School teachers, Mr. Mitchell and Faye Banks. (Above, AC/SPL; right, courtesy of the *Stuttgart Daily Leader*.)

Boy Scouts from a local troop visit the Trans-Texas Airways ticket counter at Stuttgart Municipal Airport in April 1954. The only person identified is (back center) Frank Brummitt, the city's postmaster. Trans-Texas began Stuttgart's only scheduled airline service in 1953, using DC-3 aircraft handed down by larger airlines. The route system stretched from Texas to Memphis and was truly a short-haul, point-to-point operation. Service ceased in 1958. (AC/SPL.)

The Queen Mallard Contest has been held in conjunction with the World Championship Duck Calling Contest since 1956, when it was won by Pat Peacock of Stuttgart. Entrants are selected from Grand Prairie area ladies between 16 and 21 years of age. The event pictured here dates to the late 1960s. (MAGP.)

# *Three*

# RICE AND DUCK CAPITAL

This Grand Prairie farm family and threshing crew pose proudly for the camera after finishing their work. Each of the burlap bags contains 180 pounds, or four bushels, of rice, which has been separated from the straw by the threshing machine. The bags would be sewn shut with twine and later loaded on wagons and transported to the rice mill at Stuttgart. (MAGP.)

Rice Mill A of the Stuttgart Rice Mill Company (left) was built in 1907. The rice industry grew so quickly that the company soon added Mill B when more capacity was needed. The building at far right was originally the Williamson Furniture Factory. The company leased and later sold its property to the cooperative that became Riceland Foods. Around the 1940s, Mill B

76

was demolished to make way for the current brick building, which was once used as Riceland's company headquarters. Mill A was used until spontaneous combustion caused a destructive fire in June 1963. (Courtesy of the Arkansas History Commission.)

The First Load at the new Rice Mill From Hubbard Bros. Sept. 11th 09

After only two years, Stuttgart Rice Milling Company opened a second facility in 1909, referring to it as Mill B. The first load to arrive was five bags of rice from the Hubbard brothers' farm near Stuttgart on September 11, 1909. This was approximately 20 bushels or 900 pounds of paddy rice. (MAGP.)

Even in the first days of production around Stuttgart, rice growers experienced a lengthy wait at the mills, as seen in this 1910s view of wagons in line. Each sack usually held four bushels (180 pounds) of rice, and 27.7 sacks equaled one draft (5,000 pounds), which could be pulled by one good pair of horses or mules. A one-team wagon could carry 25 sacks, while two teams handled 50. (AC/SPL.)

78

This scene from 1907 depicts an early irrigation well used in rice production. The crop required large amounts of water brought to the surface by pumps. In this era, wells were operating nearly 100 feet deep into the abundant aquifer under the Grand Prairie. The drive belt connecting the engine to the pump can be seen behind the unidentified men. (MAGP.)

Instead of today's combines that cut and thresh rice in a single process, early Grand Prairie farmers had to pull their binders through the fields by mule- or horsepower. One man drove the team and another man rode the binder. A crew followed the binder and stacked some 15 bundles together into shocks, which were allowed to dry around two weeks before threshing. (MAGP.)

An early view of rice farming on the Grand Prairie, this photograph depicts a field of cut rice stacked into shocks. One bundle would typically be spread over the top of the shock to protect the rest of the rice from rain. The shocks would be allowed to dry until optimal moisture content was reached, the length of time being dependent upon the weather. (MAGP.)

This rice threshing scene from 1915 offers a good look at the equipment in use at the time. The giant steam traction engine could pull several binders or other farm machinery. The threshing machine separated the rice bundles, blowing the straw into a stack and sending the rice out through a spout. Men would catch the rice in a four-bushel sack and sew it up for transport to the mill. (AC/SPL.)

80

This pump, made by Stuttgart's Krumpen Machine Company, is hard at work on the Selig Farm in the early days of rice production. The well-dressed group looks on, while the lady second from left has her hand on the switch. The growing of rice required large quantities of water and made dependable pumps necessary. Technology had grown from advances made in the oil industry. (MAGP.)

Standard Rice Milling Company, founded in 1916, was another early rice processor in Stuttgart. This World War I–era photograph depicts the offices and milling complex, located near Anna and Harrison Streets. When Producers Rice Mill was organized in 1943, that company acquired the Standard Mill facilities and expanded into one of the nation's largest private-label packers of rice. (MAGP.)

—1913 MODEL—

Rice cultivation has always required the use of heavy equipment on spongy, wet ground. Early growers realized that to prevent implements from bogging down, weight must be spread over a large area. One solution was a continuous track of the type then coming into military usage. This crawler-tread traction engine is an example of tank-tread technology in 1913. (Courtesy of Kay Tindall Trice.)

P.A. Yohe (left) is shown starting his new 1,800-gallon rice irrigation well around 1920 on his farm at Fairmount, north of Stuttgart. The derrick represents some of the technology then being borrowed from the oil industry in the quest for more and more water for rice growing. (Courtesy of the *Stuttgart Daily Leader*.)

In November 1920, these Stuttgart duck hunters paused on Main Street to proudly show off a nice bounty from their hunt. They are, from left to right, Matt Gengler, Louis "Red" Wilhelm, Tex Erwin, and Christy Rittman. Wilhelm would go on to win the World Championship Duck Calling Contest in 1946. (MAGP.)

This timeless scene from the first days of Grand Prairie rice farming depicts men with their oxen-drawn wagon. The stack of rice straw visible at left suggests that possibly the men have recently finished harvest. Their clothes might indicate that they posed for this photograph on a subsequent day. (MAGP.)

Krumpen Machine Company exhibited its extensive line of pumps and associated equipment for use in rice farming at the Stuttgart Fairgrounds around 1910. A close look at the bottom right of this photograph reveals a lady resetting a carnival game while a child waits. The fairgrounds were northeast of Twenty-Second and Main Streets. Early Stuttgart residents enjoyed horse racing, baseball, and other diversions there. (MAGP.)

The Crowe Drug Company clown demonstrates a Krumpen irrigation pump, probably at the Stuttgart Fairgrounds, in the 1910s. The unidentified man is wearing a bib with the wording "Use Nyal Face Cream . . . Crowe Drug Co. . . . We carry a full line of photo supplies," while his tiny umbrella shields him from the large gush of water. (MAGP.)

A display truck for Fairbanks-Morse products is parked near the company's Stuttgart offices in this undated photograph. Visible on the northeast corner of Second and Main Streets is Arkansas Grain Company, purveyors of hay, grain, and seed. Later, this building would be remodeled and occupied by the McCallister Motors Ford dealership. (Courtesy of the *Stuttgart Daily Leader*.)

This 1934 concentration of mallards on Wilcox Reservoir near Stuttgart is thought to be one of the largest ever photographed. It was estimated that some 4.5 million ducks were working the area at the time. Scenes like these were widely distributed via postcards and print journalism, and no doubt attracted countless hunters to the Grand Prairie area. (Author's collection.)

The founders of the National Duck Calling Contest pictured here are, from left to right, Dr. Harold V. Glenn, Thad S. McCollum, and Verne L. Tindall, all of Stuttgart. This early-1950s photograph shows the men standing near the competition stage at Third and Main Streets. The first contest was held in Stuttgart's Main Street on November 24, 1936, in connection with the Arkansas Rice Carnival. The contest was originated by McCollum after a dispute broke out among local duck hunters as to who was the best duck caller. A contest was created to settle the dispute. Dr. Glenn convinced American Legion Post No. 48 to sponsor the contest. The post appointed a duck calling committee of three men, with Glenn as chairman and McCollum and Arthur Shoemaker responsible for staging the event. Later, Tindall replaced Shoemaker as a committee member, and the contest was held. Thanksgiving was chosen because it occurs during Arkansas's duck season. Stuttgart benefitted greatly from the work of these Legionnaires who generated civic pride and brought in needed revenue to the area following the difficult Depression years. (Author's collection.)

The National Duck Calling Contest is in its second year in this 1937 scene. Cofounder Verne Tindall addresses the crowd and is being heard on radio stations KARK (Little Rock) and KSD (St. Louis). Looking south from Third and Main Streets, this view illustrates the popularity of the contest even in its infancy. At far right, the Riceland Hotel, Moll Appliance Shop, and Watkins Café are visible along Main Street. Below, this overhead view of the 1938 National Duck Calling Contest was photographed in the same location from a window in the Riceland Hotel. The crowd, assembled in Main Street, is listening to the program, which is being broadcast over Stuttgart, Little Rock, and St. Louis radio stations. (Both, MAGP.)

John Woerner (left), Harry Wieman (center), and Thomas E. Walsh pose with the ornament that was displayed on the duck calling contest stage in the early days. Wieman is holding a certificate from the American Legion post, indicating this photograph is from 1937 or 1938—the two years he won the contest. (MAGP.)

Louis "Red" Wilhelm is shown in a timeless waterfowl hunting setting near Stuttgart. A longtime area sportsman and booster, Wilhelm won the World Championship Duck Calling Contest in 1946. With an abundance of surface water, nutritious flooded rice fields, and a convenient location at the neck of the Mississippi Flyway, the region sees millions of migratory waterfowl winter fly over in each year. (MAGP.)

Stuttgart sportsmen Kenneth "Slick" McCollum (left) and Louis "Red" Wilhelm pose for this quintessential duck hunting publicity photograph in flooded hardwoods typical of the region. McCollum, the 1939 duck calling contest winner, owned the highly successful Stuttgart Hunting Club on Bayou Meto. Wilhelm was the 1946 world champion duck caller. Arkansas's duck hunting season begins in November, after the massive acreage of rice fields in the eastern part of the state have been harvested. Farmers flood their fields, which offsets some of the habitat decline of recent decades, giving the birds additional feeding opportunities. The Mississippi Flyway brings millions of migrating ducks and geese annually from Canada and the northern United States to southern regions. Beginning in the 1920s, photographs like these were widely circulated in print media to attract hunting enthusiasts. After the advent of radio and television, word spread rapidly of the excellent waterfowl hunting conditions around Stuttgart and East Arkansas. The state ranks no. 1 in mallards taken, and is always among the leaders in overall waterfowl harvest. (MAGP.)

Scenes such as this brought Arkansas, and the Stuttgart region in particular, much acclaim over the years as a waterfowl hunting paradise. Widely circulated in periodicals, postcards, and promotional campaigns, these types of images have delivered countless millions in revenue for the area. Waterfowl hunters continue to make Stuttgart a destination of choice for their favorite

activity. Besides natural wetlands in the form of flooded hardwoods, the Grand Prairie area is covered with rice fields that are also flooded after harvest each fall. This provides a preferred source of nutrition for the fowl, which thrive in this environment where they feed on waste grain, weed sprouts and seeds, and aquatic invertebrates. (MAGP.)

The Riceland Hotel opened in 1923 at a cost of $215,000. The five-story building had around 70 guest rooms, half of which offered private baths. All rooms had hot and cold running water and steam heat. Known for excellent food, the Riceland had a coffee shop with a street entrance, as well as a dining room off the main lobby. The latter was host to banquets and civic club meetings. The Riceland's most unique feature was its rooftop garden, one of only two in the state when built. Dances and parties were held high over street level, where patrons could have food brought up to them and dine while listening to music. Duck hunters filled the Riceland to capacity during hunting season. Guides gathered at the hotel and enlisted business from the hunters. The Riceland hosted many celebrities over its five decades of service, including publisher Joseph Pulitzer, industrialist John Olin, Gen. Jonathan Wainwright, jeweler Pierre Cartier, baseball star Ted Williams, and actors Wallace Beery, Andy Devine, and Robert Taylor. The Riceland closed its doors in 1970. (MAGP.)

This early combine, a 1940s McCormick-Deering Rice Field Special, is shown in action on the Tindall Farm near Stuttgart. In 1922, brothers Verne and Art Tindall bought land three miles south of Stuttgart. They built the first reservoir on the Grand Prairie in 1925 for irrigating rice—and "then the ducks came." Known as Sunset Farms, it is still family owned today. (MAGP.)

This view looking east from the Producers Rice Mill complex shows a full lot of trucks awaiting access to the mill in the late 1940s. Producers was organized in 1943 and expanded into cooperative rice drying in 1946. Today, it is one of the world's largest rice processors. (Courtesy of Kay Tindall Trice.)

This overhead view from around 1940 shows the Arkansas Rice Growers Cooperative Association's mill complex. Elements of the original Stuttgart Rice Milling Company are visible, such as Mill A at right. The Rock Island Railroad depot can be seen along First Street, nestled in with the elevators. A steam switch engine is working the Cotton Belt Railroad's yard at the College Street crossing at upper left. (MAGP.)

This 1940s postcard view depicts part of the rice mill complex of Arkansas Rice Growers Cooperative Association, predecessor of today's Riceland Foods. The elevators are located northwest of the First Street and Grand Avenue intersection. The scene is quite different today, with much expansion and renovation having taken place. (Author's collection.)

Aerial View of Rice Fields, Stuttgart, Arkansas

PHOTO BY OENING STUDIO

This aerial postcard image illustrates a typical Grand Prairie rice farming operation from above. The scene depicts the distinctive pattern of levees and contours necessary for water impoundment in individual fields, based on their unique landforms. Today's rice growers use equipment based upon satellite technology to obtain optimum placement of levees. (Author's collection.)

Combining Rice
near Stuttgart, Arkansas

Around the World War II years, the invention of the self-propelled combine harvester radically changed agriculture on the Grand Prairie from the labor-intensive practices of the past. Mechanization greatly increased yields and saved time, while lowering the amount of manpower needed to carry out farming activities. Today, rice ranks fifth in production value among crops grown in the United States. (Author's collection.)

The Rice Branch Experiment Station of the University of Arkansas is shown in this aerial view. The first land acquired for the station was deeded in 1927, when a group of farmers and the university recognized the need for locally conducted rice research. This nationally prominent facility would grow into today's Rice Research and Extension Center. The larger building, originally the director's home, is still standing. (MAGP.)

As part of the European Recovery Program (Marshall Plan), the American initiative to aid post–World War II Europe, the United States gave food and economic support to help rebuild economies after the war. Stuttgart and the Grand Prairie were quick to join in the effort. Pictured here around 1948, this was one of the boxcars of rice sent out for shipment to Europe. (AC/SPL.)

The duck calling contest, held each November, has seen all descriptions of weather. The event is pictured here on a wet midday around 1950, in a view looking southeast toward Fourth and Main Streets. In those days, Pulitzer-owned radio station KSD in St. Louis broadcast the contest to a wide area. Joseph Pulitzer was a frequent visitor to Stuttgart in duck season. (MAGP.)

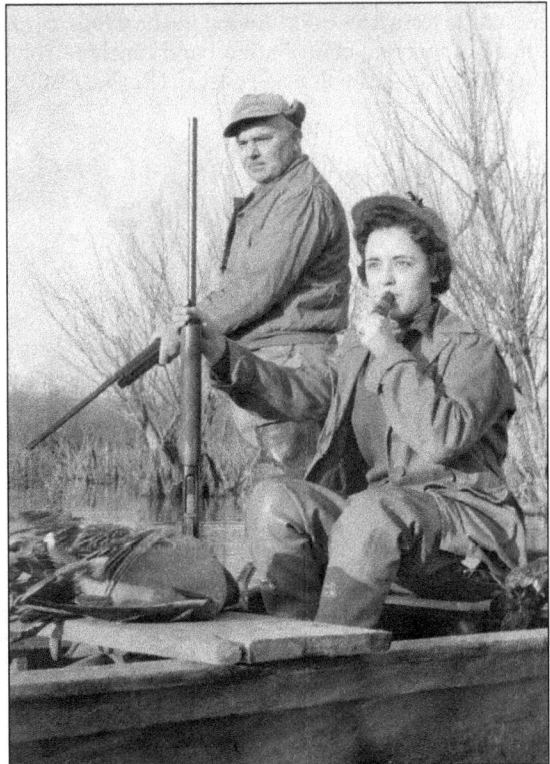

Pat Peacock (right), shown duck hunting with Henry Bennett, is recognized as the only woman in history to win the men's division of the World Championship Duck Calling Contest (1955 and 1956). She also won the 1960 men's Champion of Champions competition. Peacock won multiple women's division championships and was also the first Queen Mallard in 1956. (MAGP.)

97

The World Championship Duck Calling Contest has been held every November since 1936 and is the oldest festival in Arkansas. In this view looking north from Fourth and Main Streets in the 1950s, the contest and carnival is set up in the midst of Stuttgart's business district. The stage can be seen in the center of Main Street near the Riceland Hotel. Many typical small-town businesses of the era are shown in both images. Below, this view looking south from Third and Main Streets shows the festivities in full swing in the 1950s. Stuttgart's largest annual event remains a major source of tourism, contributing handsomely to the Grand Prairie's economy. It is today part of the Wings Over the Prairie Festival. (Both, MAGP.)

During the 1950s, a duck-picking contest was held as part of the World Championship Duck Calling Contest in Stuttgart. This scene shows several contestants in front of the stage busily plucking their birds. In this instance, the contest stage was set up in the intersection of Second and Main Streets. (MAGP.)

One rice milling firm not headquartered in Stuttgart was Texas-based Comet Rice. Its mill was located on East Nineteenth Street where it crossed the Cotton Belt Railroad's Gillett branch. The facility originally operated under the Wonder Rice brand. Shown here around 1960, the complex is still standing, although in dilapidated condition. (AC/SPL.)

Invented and manufactured by Curt Eddins of Stuttgart, the grain carts sold by Eddins Sales and Service could be found all over the Delta region on rice and soybean farms in the latter half of the 20th century. The firm began producing these and other farming accessories in 1944. (MAGP.)

This 1960s postcard view looks south toward Stuttgart's rice mills, dryers, and storage facilities. From a distance, the unique skyline resembles a much larger city. In the foreground, a rice combine harvests the golden crop in late summer. Arkansas now accounts for nearly half of the nation's rice crop. (Author's collection.)

# Four

# POSTWAR GROWTH

The post–World War II years saw a concerted effort to promote the city as a destination for business growth. Stuttgart's Chamber of Commerce and Industrial Development Corporation led the way in this push. This photograph from around 1955 captures the parade held on Industrial Appreciation Day. Leading the way is an impressive group of Boy Scouts and Cub Scouts. (AC/SPL.)

Krummen Bus Line, owned by Ed Krummen, operated to various parts of the Grand Prairie from Stuttgart. The firm opened its transportation business in 1915. Around 1929, part of the route system was contracted to Southwestern Transportation Company, a subsidiary of the Cotton Belt Railroad, to replace service on unprofitable branch rail lines such as those to Gillett and England. Krummen's buses picked up and discharged passengers in front of the Riceland Hotel at that time. Later, the stops were made at Whiteway Esso on Main Street. A typical journey on one of the four daily runs from Stuttgart to Gillett took an hour and a half, with intermediate stops at Almyra and DeWitt. This 1940s photograph depicts Krummen's fleet and drivers at the firm's general office and garage at 215 East Second Street, Stuttgart. Taxi service was also offered to local residents throughout the firm's existence. (MAGP.)

McCollum Auto Company was located at 320 South Main Street. In this 1940s view, Teddy (left) and Thad McCollum proudly display new Plymouth and DeSoto automobiles. The occasion for the flowers was possibly the company's grand opening or the introduction of a new model year. (MAGP.)

Coker-Hampton Drug Company has been in its present location since 1928. In this photograph, employees are celebrating the company's 20th anniversary in 1948. Persons pictured are, from left to right, Mac McGraw, unidentified, Tom Coker, Bill Hampton, unidentified soda fountain staff, and an unidentified radio announcer in front. (Courtesy of the *Stuttgart Daily Leader*.)

Jess Orval Dockery operated a flying service at Stuttgart for many years. A true aviation pioneer, he became one of the first pilots to dust a crop from the air in 1924 and is considered the originator of aerial rice seeding. In 1926, aged 17, Dockery flew the mail from St. Louis to Chicago with Charles Lindbergh. Once considered the top-rated stunt pilot in the nation, Dockery was equally skilled in precision aerobatics, barnstorming, flight instruction, and agricultural aviation. He became one of Braniff Airlines' first three pilots, and served as test pilot for Cessna Aircraft. He operated air charter services for over half a century without an accident or passenger injury. Irene and J.O. Dockery are shown above in 1946 with their Stearman aircraft. At left, J.O. Dockery poses next to one of his crop dusters. (Both, courtesy of Andy Holbert.)

Townsend Lumber Company is prominent in the foreground of this aerial photograph from the 1950s, with a view looking south. Its new headquarters building is seen at lower left. The new Highway 79 Bypass traverses the scene at bottom. At lower right, the new Stuttgart Motel is open for business, heralding the coming age of motor traffic bypassing traditional business districts. The motel still stands today but is hidden behind modern buildings along Highway 79. The distinctive Stuttgart grain elevator skyline dominates the background. Cotton Belt Railroad's 300-foot-long depot is visible at upper right. The railroad's Gillett branch turns to the south behind Townsend Lumber, en route to south Arkansas County. The branch was principally used to haul agricultural products to market and offered passenger service until 1928. In the 1950s, the railroad's yard facilities were located in town, as can be seen here. (MAGP.)

In 1925, prominent Stuttgart attorney Clyde Pettit established the world's first seed laboratory in the former Searan Feed Mill at 123 North College Street. The complex is pictured here in the mid-20th century, after it became Pioneer Seed Company. Although no longer at this location, the parent company is now the largest US producer of hybrid seeds for agriculture. (MAGP.)

Booker T. Releford operated the J.W. Releford and Son Funeral Home, founded by his father in 1914. The mortuary was located at 618 North Porter Street. After his father's passing in 1955, Releford served as funeral director until his death in 1983. The firm was then operated by his widow and son until recent years. (Courtesy of Mrs. B.T. Releford.)

Knoll Motors sold Packard, Willys, and Jeep vehicles at this location on the south side of Sixth Street west of Main Street. Shown here in the post–World War II years, the building later became home to the *Stuttgart Daily Leader*, which it remains today. The Standard Oil (Esso) station can be seen at left. (MAGP.)

This 1954 Oldsmobile gets intensive care from Finch's Esso Servicenter on the southwest corner of Sixth and Main Streets. Identified in the photograph are (adding air to the tire) Horace Shrum and (to his right) owner Eugene Finch. They offered the motorist "Everything You Need for Happy Motoring." (MAGP.)

This brick structure was built to house the Four States (later Southwestern States) Telephone Company. Situated on the southwest corner of Sixth and College Streets, the building later served as offices for the Macom, Moorhead, and Henry law firm, after the telephone company relocated to Seventh and College Streets. (Courtesy of the *Stuttgart Daily Leader*.)

This aerial postcard view looking east depicts Stuttgart during the 1950s, before construction of the giant Riceland Foods soybean processing facility on the city's northeast edge. The five-story Riceland Hotel is visible at far right. The Cotton Belt Railroad maintained its yard tracks west of Main Street in this era. (Author's collection.)

Once the Highway 79 Bypass was completed in the 1950s, motorists no longer needed to pass through Stuttgart's business district. To capitalize on this change, the Stuttgart Motel opened on East Michigan Avenue, drawing customers away from the downtown Riceland, Honers, and Home Hotels. The building still stands, although mostly obscured by newer businesses fronting Highway 79. (Author's collection.)

The 31-room Hanson Motel, owned and operated by Mrs. E.O. Hanson, opened in the 1950s at 200 West Michigan Avenue. The rooms were advertised as "modern, fire and sound proof, with wall to wall carpet, free TV, tub and shower bath, air conditioning and electric heating, thermostat controlled." Once Interstate 40 was completed, rerouting much of Highway 79's through traffic, Stuttgart's motels began steadily losing business. (Author's collection.)

Landrum's Pan-Am Station on the northeast corner of Main and Michigan Streets served through traffic on the newly constructed Highway 79 Bypass in the mid-1950s. The service station featured an in-house snack bar and restaurant as well as the convenient 7Up vending machine next to the entry door. (MAGP.)

This group of Stuttgart's ladies models the latest fashions offered by the Cotton Shop around 1955. They are, from left to right, (sitting) Mary Lou Harper, Genevieve Woerner, Linda Minton, Regina Jones, and Ruth Stroh; (standing) Emma Lee, Sally Jones, Shelley Simpson, Mary Linebarrier, and Ruth Cobb. (MAGP.)

McCollum Sales Company was located at 320 South Main Street in the 1940s. The firm sold radios, natural gas appliances, and Plymouth and DeSoto automobiles. Attorney William C. Gibson's practice occupied one of the upstairs offices. Sam's Department Store can be seen on the left. These three storefronts were known as the Pettit-Ellis-Nicholson Building. (Courtesy of the *Stuttgart Daily Leader*.)

The Majestic Theatre stood on the south side of Fourth Street, west of Main Street. The marquee announces the showing of *Man Who Never Was*, starring Clifton Webb, dating this scene to 1956. The Majestic was the largest and longest-operating movie theater in Stuttgart. First Federal Savings would soon be built on the corner in foreground. (MAGP.)

This view of Stuttgart was taken around the 1950s. The large complex in the foreground is the Fairbanks-Morse plant, a longtime corporate citizen of the region, makers of pumps, engines, and supplies for the rice industry. In the bottom left corner is Holy Rosary Catholic Church, at Second and Leslie Streets. The Rock Island Railroad's branch to Mesa crosses the Cotton Belt's Gillett branch in the center of the photograph. These branch lines were vital to Grand Prairie farming interests in the days before highway trucks began doing most of the hauling. The large milling complexes of Arkansas Rice Growers Cooperative Association and Producers Rice Mill (top center) dominate the scene at top. Rice is the fifth-largest crop in the United States, while Arkansas accounts for nearly half of that production. Rice farming and processing contributes some $6 billion to the state's economy. (MAGP.)

Hartz Seed Company was founded around 1942 by Jacob Hartz Sr. The firm became a leader in research of new seed varieties, crop improvement, and market development. In 1925, Hartz was first to implement planting of the soybean as a viable crop in Arkansas, leading to an industry that today is a $500 million cash crop, with over three million acres grown annually. Hartz Seed's dryer is pictured around the 1950s. (MAGP.)

The Stuttgart Post Office at Third and Maple Streets, opened in 1932, was built at a cost of $60,000. In 1968, an addition was built onto the north side of the structure. This post office served the region well for 70 years before being replaced in 2002. Stuttgart City Hall now occupies the nicely restored building. (AC/SPL.)

Herman Freeman Buick Company, shown here in a mid-1950s photograph, faced west near the northeast corner of Second Street and Grand Avenue. The building is of a utilitarian type, with a modern facade added onto a military surplus Quonset hut, quite possibly acquired from Stuttgart Army Airfield upon its closure. (MAGP.)

The Grand Prairie War Memorial Auditorium, built in the late 1950s, served as a National Guard armory as well as meeting place for many area functions. The building at Twentieth and Columbus Streets hosted school graduations, plays, and other programs needing a stage and sound system. It suffered heavy damage in a 2008 tornado and was partially rebuilt. A new armory was constructed at Stuttgart Municipal Airport. (AC/SPL.)

Beginning in 1931, the Cotton Belt Railroad operated some of the fastest freight schedules in the nation. The railroad company called its highest priority train the Blue Streak. In the early 1930s, the train operated from East St. Louis to Pine Bluff. Then in 1935, the train was extended to Dallas and Fort Worth. Plans to operate the Blue Streak all the way to Los Angeles over the parent Southern Pacific Railroad were shelved during the World War II years, as railroads struggled to handle the unprecedented volume of traffic. By 1946, the Cotton Belt was running its renamed Blue Streak Merchandise from East St. Louis to Los Angeles. Shown here passing Stuttgart southbound in the 1950s, this Cotton Belt train likely originated at East St. Louis and carried everything from automobile parts to small express shipments bound for Texas or California markets. The railroad ran several sections of the Blue Streaks as well as other fast trains. (Author's collection.)

Main Motor Company was a Dodge and Plymouth dealership located on the southwest corner of Seventh and Main Streets. In this late-1950s view, a Mobilgas pump is barely visible along the building's wall to the right. The building was acquired by Farmers and Merchants Bank in 1958, and after extensive renovation is still the bank's main location. (MAGP.)

Walton's Esso Servicenter, shown here in the mid-1950s, was built on the southwest corner of Main and Michigan Streets to capitalize on the growing traffic flow around Stuttgart on the Highway 79 Bypass. The station, originally operated by Thomas Walton, would survive until well into the 2000s due to its good location. (MAGP.)

Stuttgart City Hall and Fire Station are pictured in this postcard view from around 1960. The new city hall (left) was built in 1958 and joined onto the existing fire department building. The original part of the fire station dates back to the early 1900s. A second story was added around 1929. The station was again enlarged in 1958. (Author's collection.)

The Arkansas County Courthouse at Third and College Streets was built in 1928 to replace the frame building at Fourth and Leslie Streets, which was demolished to make way for the Julia Shannon Grade School. Arkansas County was split into two judicial districts in 1913, with court for the northern district originally being held in the former Stuttgart Public School. (Author's collection.)

Cotton Belt train No. 7 calls at Stuttgart for the final time at 8:30 a.m. on November 30, 1959. Originating at East St. Louis, the train terminated at Pine Bluff, ending the rail line's passenger service after 76 years. Beginning in the 1930s, the Cotton Belt's principal passenger train services were called Lone Star Trains and ran out of St. Louis and Memphis to Dallas and Fort Worth with connecting service to Shreveport and Texas cities such as Tyler and Waco. Generally, one train was operated to and from St. Louis, with two trains in and out of Memphis. Declining post–World War II revenues led railroads to reduce or drop service beginning in the late 1950s. As a result, Cotton Belt's trains in the last decade of service usually consisted of a baggage car, mail car, and coach. (Courtesy of the *Stuttgart Daily Leader*.)

Cotton Belt depot agent Roy Pullig is shown on the last day of passenger service in 1959, with a roll of tickets he would no longer need. When Pullig began work in the 1920s, 10 trains a day operated through Stuttgart. But Cotton Belt's passenger revenues had dropped to $91,000 in 1958, after wartime highs of $4.4 million. (Author's collection.)

Pictured here in the 1960s, the handsome Mission Revival–style Cotton Belt Railroad depot opened in 1910. For a time, passengers could board trains destined for Texas, St. Louis, Memphis, Gillett, North Little Rock, and Hazen. Passenger service ended in 1959. The depot was demolished in 1987 after the railroad no longer needed the structure. (Author's collection.)

Stuttgart Memorial Hospital opened in the late 1950s on North Buerkle Road, answering the city's need for intensive health care following the closure of the Eileen Drennen Hospital. The new hospital was built on part of a former golf course, adjacent to Gum Pond and the Mitchell Plantation site. (Author's collection.)

Stuttgart Public Library opened this modern building on the southwest corner of Fourth Street and Grand Avenue in the early 1960s. Visible behind the library is the tower of St. John's Lutheran Church. The need for more space later led to construction of a larger library on South Buerkle Street. (MAGP.)

Typical of America's small-town atmosphere in the post–World War II era, this view from around 1960 shows the west side of Main Street near Third Street. Businesses visible are, from left to right, a ladies' fashion shop, bookshop, café, department store, dime store, hotel, bank, chamber of commerce, two jewelry stores, a pharmacy, hardware and furniture store, and pool hall. There were at least seven eating places on Main Street in this era, including three cafés, three drugstore fountains, and the Riceland Hotel Coffee Shop. Three more eateries were located within two blocks of Main Street. By this time, downtown Stuttgart had already been bypassed by Highway 79. The hotel was closed in 1970 due to declining patronage. By the late 1970s, the effects could be readily seen, as more businesses had closed or relocated to the city's outskirts. (AC/SPL.)

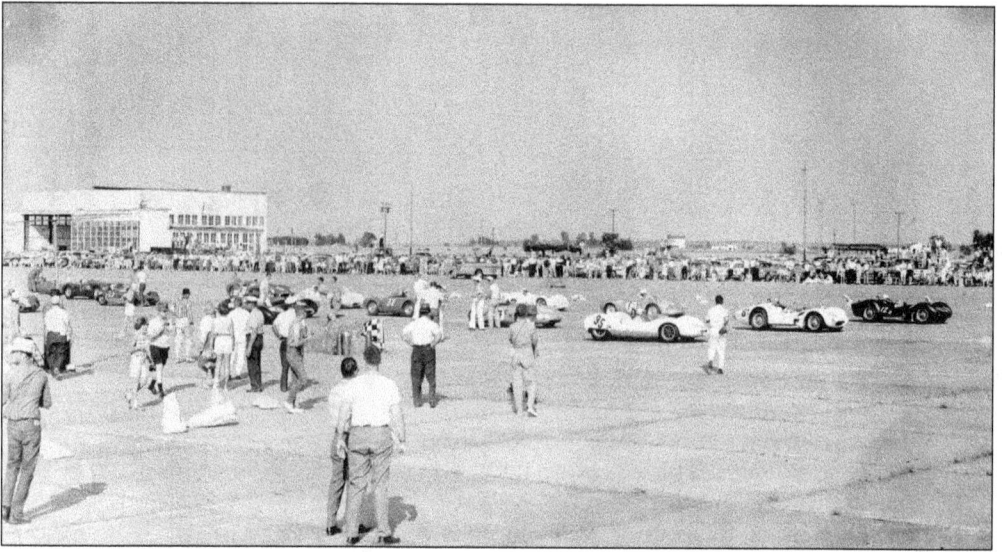

The Grand Prairie Grand Prix auto race was held at Stuttgart Municipal Airport from 1959 until 1978. The three-mile Sports Car Club of America road course was designed using the runways and aprons of the former World War II air base. This photograph shows the start of a race in the early 1960s. Below, several dignitaries are gathered in the scorer's stand at an early-1960s grand prix. They are, from left to right, (standing) Guy Martin and Chuck Ratcliff; (sitting) unidentified, Stuttgart mayor John Bueker, Arkansas governor Orval Faubus, unidentified scorer, and Dr. Jim Bisbee. (Both, courtesy of Lynn Keller.)

The swimming pool at John Cain Park is shown in this postcard view from the 1960s. The park was founded in 1938, and in later years, playground equipment, tennis courts, a concession stand, and a baseball stadium were added. The pool was located along Vine Street near the main entrance to the park. (Author's collection.)

The Home Hotel was built around 1918 as Stuttgart City Hospital. It was managed by Mrs. Rex B. Wilcox, who came from Baroness Erlanger Hospital in Chicago. The building later housed Stuttgart Sanitarium. In the mid-20th century, the Home Hotel occupied it. Damaged heavily by a severe storm, it was razed in the 1990s. The building was at 501 South Main Street. (AC/SPL.)

The intersection of Fourth and Main Streets was always a focal point of much of Stuttgart's commerce. In this late-1960s postcard view of the east side of Main Street are, from right to left, Billy's Record Shop/Word Jewelers, Peoples National Bank, Sterling Store, Belk-Jones Department Store, Moll's TV and Appliance, Pastime Pool Hall, Horst Rexall Drugs, Crowe Drugs, and West Brothers Department Store. (Author's collection.)

Shortly before its closure and subsequent demolition, Stuttgart High School is pictured here in the 1960s. The school opened in 1912, occupying a block of Ninth Street between Lowe and Buerkle Streets. Until 1928, the school housed all grades of the town's white students. The seniors of 1967 were the final class to graduate. (Author's collection.)

124

As this book comes to a close, it seems appropriate to include a couple of modern-day aerial images of the subject from the camera of Stuttgart photographer Bill Bracewell. In this view looking east toward the city, the distinctive grain elevator skyline provides a backdrop for a southbound flight of geese. Thousands more of the waterfowl have landed and are working the water impoundments at lower left. This scene illustrates the relationship between the Grand Prairie, its location on the lower end of the Mississippi Flyway, the rice industry and its impact upon the ready availability of food for migratory waterfowl, and the flat landform with its abundant wetlands. Much has changed in the Stuttgart area since Rev. Adam Buerkle brought his Lutheran colony here in 1878. Today's farming practices and crop yields would be unimaginable to the Grand Prairie's pioneers. Waterfowl populations declined to a point of concern by the mid-20th century. Conservation efforts by such groups as Ducks Unlimited have restored numbers to a desirable, sustainable level. The Stuttgart area has solidified its status as the "Rice and Duck Capital of the World." (Courtesy of Bill Bracewell.)

This aerial photograph of Stuttgart depicts today's concentration of rice milling facilities. A comparison to the image on page 108 illustrates the growth of the city and its main industry since the 1950s. Today's bustling community of around 9,500 would scarcely be recognizable to its early colonists, promoters, and citizens. The surrounding prairie grasses of the late 1800s have been replaced by rice, soybeans, corn, and other crops. World-class waterfowl hunting draws crowds of hunting enthusiasts from all over the nation. The modern city boasts a two-year college, a new multiuse convention center and auditorium, three separate research labs conducting work on rice and aquaculture, two of the nation's largest rice millers and processors, a large manufacturer of heating and cooling systems, the world's largest outfitter of waterfowl hunting gear, and a museum with over 10,000 artifacts conserving Grand Prairie heritage. (Courtesy of Bill Bracewell.)

# BIBLIOGRAPHY

Burkett, Bennie Frownfelter. *Stuttgart, Arkansas: One Hundred Years on the Grand Prairie*. Stuttgart, AR: Standard Printing Company, 1980.

*Grand Prairie Historical Bulletin*. Gillett, AR: Grand Prairie Historical Society, 1958–present.

Hanley, Steven and Ray. *Arkansas County*. Charleston, SC: Arcadia Publishing, 2008.

Stuttgart Daily Leader. *Pictorial History of the Arkansas Grand Prairie*. Marceline, MO: D-Books Publishing, 2008.

———. *Reflections of Arkansas County*. Marceline, MO: D-Books Publishing, 1995.

Visit us at
arcadiapublishing.com

www.ingramcontent.com/pod-product-compliance
Lightning Source LLC
Chambersburg PA
CBHW050559110426
42813CB00008B/2402